All About Eve

Ten Selected Women Of The Bible

Robert L. Allen

CSS Publishing Company, Inc., Lima, Ohio

ALL ABOUT EVE

Copyright © 2001 by
CSS Publishing Company, Inc.
Lima, Ohio

All rights reserved. No part of this publication may be reproduced in any manner whatsoever without the prior permission of the publisher, except in the case of brief quotations embodied in critical articles and reviews. Inquiries should be addressed to: Permissions, CSS Publishing Company, Inc., P.O. Box 4503, Lima, Ohio 45802-4503.

Scripture quotations are from the *New Revised Standard Version of the Bible*, copyright 1989 by the Division of Christian Education of the National Council of the Churches of Christ in the USA. Used by permission.

Library of Congress Cataloging-in-Publication Data

Allen, Robert L., 1946-
   All about Eve : ten selected women of the Bible / Robert L. Allen.
      p.   cm.
   ISBN 0-7880-1785-3 (pbk. : alk. paper)
   1. Women in the Bible. I. Title.
BS575 .A45 2001
220.9'2'082—dc21   00-046840
                                                                                       CIP

For more information about CSS Publishing Company resources, visit our website at www.csspub.com.

ISBN 0-7880-1785-3   PRINTED IN U.S.A.

*This book is gratefully dedicated to
Madalyne Marie Allen,
a woman of faith with whom I
have been privileged to share
my life across the years.*

Table Of Contents

Preface — 7

Chapter One — 9
All About Eve
Genesis 2:21-25; 3:1-7

Chapter Two — 15
A Biblical Soap Opera
Genesis 15:1-5

Chapter Three — 21
The Risks Of Life
Genesis 24:42-44, 55-58

Chapter Four — 27
Don't Look Back!
Genesis 19:26; 10:24-26

Chapter Five — 33
A Mixed-Up Story
Genesis 29:15-30

Chapter Six — 39
Letters In The Sand
John 8:1-11

Chapter Seven — 45
Be All That You Can Be
Luke 7:36-50

Chapter Eight   51
    Great Things In Unexpected Moments
    John 4:5-30

Chapter Nine   57
    The Touch Of Faith
    Mark 5:25-34

Chapter Ten   63
    The Touch Of Human Kindness
    Matthew 8:14-15

Preface

One day I was sitting in a meeting where a young woman was being interviewed about her decision to enter the ordained ministry. When asked why she was going into the ministry, she replied: "I believe God is calling me into the ministry. All through the Bible there have been women whose lives inspired faith. I want my life to inspire others in faith."

These words sparked my thinking. As you read through the Bible, there are so many stories of women. Perhaps it was time for me to look a little more closely at these women and how their stories have influenced our faith. As you read through this book, you will learn about women whose names were well known, such as Eve, Sarah, and Hagar. In addition, you will read about women whose names have long been forgotten.

These women of the Bible have remarkable stories. In fact, their stories are among the most exciting in all literature. As we walk through this biblical portrait gallery, we will discover women whose stories are several thousand years old, but they still share a common humanity with each of us.

Robert L. Allen

Chapter One
All About Eve

Genesis 2:21-25; 3:1-7

Imagine a minister who is close to retirement age. He has had a distinguished career, but now he is looking forward to retirement. He is looking forward to taking life easier. He is looking forward to retirement because he knows he is getting forgetful when he stands in the pulpit.

To aid in his memory lapses, he begins typing out his sermons and putting them in a three-ring binder notebook. When he walks into the pulpit, he opens his notebook and reads his sermon verbatim.

One Sunday, just as the choir finishes their beautiful anthem, he picks up his notebook and walks to the pulpit. On the way to the pulpit a page slips out of his notebook. It floats majestically to the floor — and the minister never notices.

When he reached the pulpit, he opens his notebook and begins to read his sermon. His sermon is about the creation story. When he comes to the end of a page, he reads: "And Adam looked at Eve and said ..." He turns the page ... but the page is missing. He is confused and says again: "And Adam looked at Eve and said ..." The minister scratches his head and says, "You know there must be a leaf missing."

The Scripture from Genesis is one of the great stories of the Bible. It was written to try to answer questions like: Where did life come from? Or, when did life start?

As we read the creation story, the central idea is that God created man in his own image. But, like great art, we will never understand it completely. However, there is a leaf missing, if we do not understand that women were also created in the image of God. The Scripture says: "So, God created man in his own image, in the image of God he created him; male and female he created them...." A bumper sticker I saw recently, was a little more direct. It said: "God created man, then she had a better idea."

The creation of women was not an addendum or an afterthought. Men and women were special creations and humankind was not given dominion over creation until Eve was created. The magnificent theme of creation is that Eve, whose name means "life," was created to share life with the man, Adam.

The essence of this story is that Adam and Eve were made to share life together in the Garden of Eden. They were told: "Do whatever you want in the garden except eat of the fruit of the tree of knowledge...." The Bible doesn't call it an apple tree; it simply refers to it as the *forbidden fruit*.

Then one day, Eve had a conversation with a snake. The snake, representing temptation said: "Eat the fruit of the tree. What can it hurt?" Eve considered this and one day the forbidden fruit seemed to be so tempting — so luscious — so inviting. Eve reached up and plucked the forbidden fruit and she ate. She gave some to Adam and he ate.

Immediately, they both felt guilty. They were ashamed of their nakedness and tried to hide from the presence of God. Guilt always makes us realize the wrong we have done. But where can we hide? The simple truth is that we cannot run or hide from the guilt within ourselves.

But Adam and Eve tried. They made fig-leaf aprons to cover themselves. Then they hid in the bushes, thinking they could hide from God. But they could not!

The voice of God called out: "Adam, where are you?"

And Adam said: "I was afraid and tried to hide."

And God asked: "Why did you try to hide? Have you eaten from the forbidden tree?"

Look at what Adam did; he made an excuse. He said to God: "Hey, it wasn't my fault. The woman you gave me told me to eat of the fruit of that tree." I'll bet every chance Adam had for a happy honeymoon ended with those words, don't you?

Then God asked Eve: "Why did you do this?"

Eve learned from Adam and passed the blame. She said: "Hey, it's not my fault either. It's the snake's fault!"

I suppose people need a snake on which to blame their misdeeds in life. Isn't it interesting how their guilt was handled? Adam points his finger at Eve and blames her. Eve points at the snake and blames the snake — and God banishes them from the Garden of Eden. Paradise was lost because temptation became such a strong desire in their lives, that they gave in to that which they knew to be wrong.

Even though Eve fell short of her potential and was banished from the Garden, she was the biblical foremother of our faith. When the writer of the Gospel of Matthew traces the ancestry of Jesus, he traces it back to Eve's son, Seth. In spite of her sin in the Garden, Eve still stands as a special creation of God. She learned to live life with the hand she was dealt. She was a woman who still influences our faith.

Today, as we look at Eve, the first woman, we need to be aware that she is not the reason that Paradise was lost. So, whom do we blame for losing the Garden of Eden? Who is at fault for humanity being evicted from the Garden? Do we blame Adam or Eve? The snake? Everybody and nobody?

When we are honest, all of us are just as responsible as Adam and Eve. After all, this world in which we live is a Garden of Eden, but so often we have made it into our own private hell. We give in to that which we know is wrong; we choose to walk our own path instead of God's; we evict ourselves from Eden; and we evict ourselves from the peace of the Garden.

Today, as we look at Eve, there are some ideas which are important. They are important because they are issues we are still dealing with today.

I. The First Thing To Notice In Dealing With Eve Is That Temptation Is A Reality In Life

According to the story, God told Adam and Eve that they could eat of any tree in the garden — except one. But God created us with free will. God will not force anyone to obey him. God did not force Adam and Eve, and God will not force you or me.

Likewise, God will not shield or protect us from temptation. The sin is not in being tempted because we are all tempted. The sin is in yielding to temptation. This is the battleground where we all find ourselves. Temptation is the point where we all face choices;

temptation is the point where we are confronted with choices between right and wrong.

So, Eve was tempted. The snake approached her in the garden and said: "Doesn't that fruit look good? Go ahead and eat. What could it hurt?" And we can be sure that it was a battle. The most decisive battles of history are always fought on the inner battlefield. Temptation is a reality in life and it can become a raging battlefield within as we struggle and wrestle with the choice of what is right and wrong. But after giving in to temptation one time, we are more susceptible the next time. Once we reach out for the forbidden fruit, we discover how easy it is to hang around the bargain basement counters of sin.

A man whom I know is only in his early forties. He is successful in business, he is articulate, he can afford to travel to all the popular ski areas, and he does. He has a pleasant personality, and he is a likeable person. He has everything going for him. Except he is not happy. He says the one thing he wants is a loving wife and a happy home. Yet he has been married four times. He says that each marriage goes well for a while, but then temptation comes his way in the form of an attractive woman. Desire and temptation begin raging through his mind and he gives in to the temptation. He unbridles his passion and he chooses the path which destroys his marriage.

Make no mistake about it. Temptation is a reality in life and it is a warfare waging inside our hearts and minds. Give in to it just once, partake of the forbidden fruit only one time, choose what is wrong instead of what is right, and we discover, like Eve, that we have destroyed our own Eden.

II. The Second Thing To Notice In Dealing With Eve Is That We Like To Have Someone To Blame

Adam and Eve were told they could eat of every tree in the garden except for one. And it was this one that they began to desire. The snake came along and told Eve, "Go ahead, eat the fruit. What can it hurt?"

So Eve ate of the fruit of the forbidden tree. She knew it was wrong! Guilt overwhelmed her! She was asked, "Eve, why did you do this?" She responded by saying, "Lord, it's not my fault. It's the snake's fault."

That is so typical of each of us. We do something wrong and are asked to explain our actions. What do we do? We like to have someone else to blame. We need a scapegoat (scapesnake) upon whom to blame our misdeeds. We all do it periodically, don't we?

Not long ago, a man told me about putting his two boys to bed. Apparently, five-year-old Joshua went right to sleep, but Jason, the three-year-old, was not a bit sleepy. He got up and began prowling around. First he played with toys in his bedroom. Then he wandered into his parents' bedroom while they were still in the den watching television.

As he rummaged around in his parents' bedroom, he found some jars of finger paint. He loved to fingerpaint and he began painting everything in sight: the dresser, the bed, and of course, he did a beautiful mural across the wall. Just about the time the boy was finishing his artwork, the father walked into the room and saw the mess. Fingerpaint on the walls, the furniture, and the little boy. The father, in a stern voice, asked, "Jason, what on earth are you doing?"

Realizing he was caught in the act, the little three-year-old boy looked up at his father and blamed it on his brother: "Joshua made me do it!"

Whom do you blame when things like that happen in life? We like to have someone to blame, don't we? We like to share the fault with others.

Ultimately, the responsibility for our actions rests with ourselves. When you do something wrong, accept the responsibility. Don't try to blame someone else. That doesn't solve the problem.

III. The Last Thing To Notice In Dealing With Eve Is That We Are Never Cast Out Of God's Presence

Because of the choices they made, Adam and Eve lost their Garden of Eden. Although they were evicted from Eden, they were not evicted from the presence of God. Eve gave birth to three sons, Cain, Abel, and Seth. The ancestry of Jesus was traced back to the genealogy of Seth, the third son of Adam and Eve.

They lost Eden, but they did not lose the presence of God. I wonder if we can ever really grasp the significance of this. We are privileged to live in this world that God has given us. But like Adam and Eve, we sometimes make it a hell. But God is still with us. God does not leave us; God does not condemn us; God does not punish us; God is with us. God is trying to help us build a paradise of our own personal world.

Mark Twain wrote a beautiful little short story titled, "The Diary of Adam and Eve." It is a delightful and humorous story in which Mark Twain portrays Adam as an obnoxious, insensitive, and arrogant individual. He portrays Adam as the kind of man that everyone wants to avoid.

However, at the end of the short story, Adam is standing beside Eve's grave. There is grief and pain in Adam's heart as he says: "Wheresoever she was, there was Eden."

I am not sure we will ever fully understand the love of God for each of us. Jesus spent his life trying to help us understand the height, length, depth, and breadth of his love. God is not against us and we cannot be evicted from God's presence ... we cannot be evicted from God's love ... we cannot do anything that will separate us from God's love. This is the Good News!

God is with us — even now — urging us to make an Eden of the world in which we live.

Prayer

O God, we give you thanks for your love which never leaves us because of your Son, Jesus Christ. In his name. Amen.

Chapter Two
A Biblical Soap Opera
Genesis 15:1-5

A cartoon in a newspaper shows two women sitting at their office desks. One looks at the other and says, "So, how do you like your job?"

"I love it!" the other responds. "When I wasn't working, all I did was lounge around the house and watch soap operas."

"Me, too!" the other woman said.

The last panel shows each woman thinking to herself, "Now, I tape them."

Since the earliest days of television, one of the most popular program formats has been the soap opera. There have been shows like *Search For Tomorrow, All My Children, As The World Turns, Dallas, Dynasty,* and *The Guiding Light.*

Why is it that soap operas have been so popular? I suppose it is because they are stories filled with jealousy and revenge, love and sex, anger and bitterness. Every soap opera has these emotions, and we identify with them. Perhaps that's why they are so popular!

The Scripture today is about two women of the Bible, Sarah and Hagar. It is a marvelous story having all the key elements of a biblical soap opera. Sarah was married to Abraham, a man who was promised that he would be the father of a great nation. Sarah had many admirable qualities. Apparently, she was a beautiful woman because the Bible describes her as "a fair woman to look upon." On two occasions a king of some province wanted to add the radiantly beautiful Sarah to his harem. But Sarah loved Abraham and her love could not be bought with the riches and the power and the luxuries a king could provide. She chose with her heart and stayed with Abraham.

Although Sarah had many admirable qualities, the great tragedy of her life was that she did not have a son. During this period in history, a woman's importance and value in life was in whether or not she gave birth to a son. It was through a son that a man lived on into the future.

The failure to give birth to a son was a painful thing for Sarah. She felt guilty about not bearing a son. A sense of shame overwhelmed her. She became almost paranoid about wanting a son for her husband.

So, one day, Sarah told Abraham that she wanted him to go and sleep with the Egyptian handmaiden, Hagar. Sarah hoped that Hagar would become pregnant and that she would give birth to a son. Then Abraham would have his heir — a son to continue his name.

Although not stated in the Bible, Abraham seemed rather quick to participate voluntarily in this proposal. With a lecherous grin on his face, he made his way to Hagar's tent. Hagar did conceive and bore a son who was named Ishmael.

For a while, everything seemed to be fine. Sarah was satisfied with Abraham having a son by a surrogate mother. But then one day Sarah realized she was to have a child. It was a boy whom they named Isaac. Shortly after the birth of Isaac, Sarah began to simmer with jealously. The idea that sounded so good in the beginning was now filling her with jealousy. Her son Isaac was now second in line to his father's inheritance. By law, Ishmael would receive two-thirds and her son Isaac only one-third of the inheritance. So she said to Abraham: "I will not have Ishmael inherit anything that belongs to my son!"

Jealousy and anger became rampant in her heart. She could no longer call Hagar by her name. Sarah called her "That woman," or "that Egyptian woman." You can almost feel the heat of Sarah's anger as she says: "Cast out this slave woman and her son!"

Reluctantly, Abraham gave some bread and water to Hagar and Ishmael and sent them out into the wilderness. Talk about being henpecked! Abraham was willing to send his son and lover out into the wilderness with only bread and water. What a character problem he had! Abraham knew his son would get hungry. What was Hagar to do? Stop at the country club for brunch? Walk up to a grocery store and get the food she and Ishmael would need?

Abraham watched them walk off into that desolate wilderness and he knew his son and his lover would probably die.

This story has all of the drama of a soap opera. There is love and sex and guilt; there is jealousy, pain, and heartache; there is tragedy, intrigue, and human emotion. It has all the makings of a soap opera, but change a few details and it might be our story. After all, haven't we all laid out plans only to have them blow up in our faces?

Today, I want to look at how this biblical soap opera involving these two women, Sarah and Hagar, applies to our lives.

I. The Biblical Soap Opera Of Sarah And Hagar Is A Story Of Relationships

We cannot help but find ourselves in the story of Sarah and Hagar. The push and pull of human relationships remind us not only that we need each other, but that we can be the most cruel to those with whom we are closest. Did you see what O. J. Simpson was quoted as saying? He said: "Let's say I committed this crime. Even if I did do this, it would have to have been because I loved her very much." Pretty sick, isn't it? But the sad fact is that we often treat those who are closest to us the most cruelly.

We see that happen in Sarah's changing feelings about Hagar and Ishmael. Hagar trusted Sarah, but Sarah wanted her sent away. Hagar had not done anything wrong. Hagar tended to Sarah's needs; Hagar bore a son for Sarah's husband; Hagar was close to Sarah and vulnerable to Sarah's wrath.

Why is it that we undermine those who are close to us? Why is that we try to put down those who are close to us? Why is it we are willing to hurt those who are close to us?

A man who had virtually nothing married a very wealthy woman. But she had a cruel streak in her and liked to remind him that she was the one with the money. When they moved into a new house, she said, "Now, George, without my money, we wouldn't be here."

When the new furniture was delivered, she said, "Now, George, without my money, this furniture wouldn't be here."

When they took a cruise, she said, "George, without my money, we wouldn't be here."

But he cut her short one day when he said, "Honey, always remember that without your money, I wouldn't be here!"

God meant for us to live in a loving and caring relationship with one another. But far too often we vent our anger at those closest to us. We allow our emotions to explode and we lash out at those we claim to care about. We strike out and try to put down those who mean so much to us.

Why do we do this?

The next time your emotions begin to consume you and you are feeling like hurting someone with your words and your actions, take a time-out. You don't really want to hurt those who are close to you, so why do it?

II. The Biblical Soap Opera Of Sarah And Hagar Is A Story Of One Taking Advantage Of Another

There is little doubt that Sarah took advantage of Hagar. Although women did not have a place of importance in society 3,000 to 4,000 years ago, they did have a position of importance in the family. Sarah was the wife of Abraham and Hagar was only a slave, a servant who assisted Sarah, a handmaiden, and a concubine for Abraham.

Sarah was holding all the aces and she knew it. She confronted Abraham with the demand: "Get rid of that Egyptian woman."

Abraham did not want to cast out Hagar and his son. But he could not challenge Sarah's position of authority over a slave woman. So he cast them out into the wilderness. He sent them out with only bread and water. He did not care what happened to them; he was thinking only of himself.

We have a tendency of taking advantage of others, don't we? We are aware that we had better watch out or someone will pull a fast one on us. And, none of us likes to be cheated.

David Read was a chaplain in the British Army during World War II. He was taken prisoner at the Battle of Dunkirk. He was put in a POW camp and shared a hut with eight other chaplains. The food they were fed by the Nazis was revolting. Yet, they counted the hours until it arrived each day. He said, "We took turns dishing it out. One day, one of the chaplains jumped to his feet and said: 'I can't stand it anymore. Here we are, ordained ministers of the church, chaplains in His Royal Majesty's Army, and we are all sitting here with our eyes fixed upon that bucket to make sure no one gets one teaspoon more than we do.' "

We know that to be true! We have all fallen into the trap of "me first." We have all been in the position where we had the upper hand and we took advantage of that position to put ourselves first. We have a tendency to look out for ourselves, to take care of ourselves.

And there is nothing wrong with this as long as we don't take advantage of someone else, as long as we don't deliberately hurt someone else, as long as we don't hurt someone else by putting ourselves first.

III. The Biblical Story Of Sarah And Hagar Is A Story About God Helping His People

God's help does not always come in the way we want or expect it, but it always comes. Hagar and Ishmael were cast out into the wilderness. As far as the eye could see, there was the desert. Above the desert, you could see the heat waves dancing. The wind whipped up little whirling dust devil funnels, and there was not an oasis in sight. The only visible protection from the sun was a few scraggy bushes.

The silence of the desert was broken by a small boy's whimpering and Hagar's weeping. The food and water were gone and the boy, Ishmael, is close to death. There is no pain like the pain of a mother watching her child die. Hagar thought she was alone, abandoned, forgotten. But suddenly, in the midst of her grief, she heard the voice of God say: "Hagar, why you are troubled? Don't be afraid ... pick up the boy and comfort him. I will make a great nation out of his descendants."

Hagar had wandered over the hot desert. She was lost and had no way of knowing where she was, but she had not traveled beyond God's knowledge. She had not traveled beyond God's presence. Hagar had lost herself, but God had not lost Hagar. And there in the wilderness, she discovered a spring of water and she and her son survived.

God's help always comes. It may not be in the way we want it or expect it, but God never leaves us lost and alone in the wilderness.

Chuck Colson, the White House lawyer who went to prison because of his participation in Watergate, said:

> *I had arrived at everything I had ever dreamed about as a kid. I was 41 years old, had a yacht in the Chesapeake Bay, and I was Special Counsel to the President of the United States of America ... Then I was arrested, tried, and sent to prison. I had never felt more rotten and abandoned in my life. Then one day in that prison, I realized I was not alone or abandoned. God was there with me and this became the most pervasive truth of my life....*

Take a moment and look back over your life. You have been lost in the wilderness of life at some time or another. There have been many times when you have felt alone and abandoned. There have been times when you could see no way out. But then you begin to pray; you look to seek God's help. And slowly, but surely, you begin to realize that God is there with you, promising to never ever leave you alone.

Whether you know it or not, at this moment God is with you and ready to help. God's help may not come in the way you want or expect it, but just as God was there to help Hagar in the wilderness, God is there with you in your wilderness.

Is there some problem that has left you weeping and alone in the wilderness?

Is there some knot which seems to have your life hopelessly tangled?

Is there some pain which has left your heart aching?

The Good News of the gospel is that God has not left you alone or abandoned. Jesus said to his disciples, and to you and me: "Lo, I am with you always!"

Do you know that God, through Jesus Christ, is with you?

Prayer

O God, we are grateful that your loving Presence is always with us. In Jesus' name. Amen.

Chapter Three
The Risks Of Life

Genesis 24:42-44, 55-58

The story came out of Washington, D.C., and spread around the world with incredible speed. A feeding frenzy of reporters serving up tidbits of news and unidentified sources liberally using the words like "affair" and "perjury" and "impeachment," and lawyers speaking of "obstruction of justice" and "immunity from prosecution" in exchange for sworn testimony.

This has been our news for the past several days. The Pope's trip to Cuba has been all but forgotten, the Oprah trial about beef infected with mad-cow disease has been virtually ignored, Sadaam Hussein and his refusal to allow United Nations inspectors to search for weapons of mass destruction has been pushed out of our minds.

The major news story for the past several days has been the alleged sexual affair the President of the United States reportedly had with a White House intern. One person, trying to sum up what is being reported, put it very clearly: "At this moment, the life of a presidency is hanging on a laundry line of 'ifs.' If it can be proved that the charges are false, it is the worst smear of a President in history. However, if it can be proved that the charges are true and that President Clinton lied under oath and urged others to perjure themselves, then Bill Clinton has put his presidency at risk."

Whether we like it or not, life is filled with risks. And this is why the story about Rebekah, one of the women of the Bible, is so appealing. Rebekah had many admirable qualities because she was friendly, helpful, courteous, industrious, and very attractive. But her most interesting trait was that she knew life involved a certain amount of risk. She was willing to weigh the risks that came her way in life.

Abraham wanted a wife for his son, Isaac. Abraham did not want Isaac to take a wife from the Caananites where they lived. So he sent his trusted servant back to the land of Ur of the Chaldees to find a wife among Abraham's people.

The servant made the long journey to Abraham's homeland. When he finally arrived, he went to the local well where young women would come to draw water. Then the servant devised a plan for finding a wife for Isaac. He prayed: "O God, grant me success today. Let the maiden to whom I shall say, 'Pray, let down your jar that I may drink,' and who shall say, 'Drink and I will water your camels' — let her be the one whom you have appointed for Isaac...."

Do you believe that God is interested in whom you marry? Do you believe that God will guide you in the selection of a husband or wife?

Perhaps you think falling in love is enough. But so often we confuse love with sexual attraction. My advice to young people is to seek God's help and guidance. Just as God guides you in all areas of your life, God will guide you in finding someone to love and share your life.

In this biblical story, Abraham's servant met Rebekah at the well. She not only gave the man a drink, but she also drew water for his camels. This convinced the servant that he had found the woman to be the wife of Isaac.

The scene that followed moved rapidly. Abraham's servant explained his mission to Rebekah's family. He gave lavish gifts to the family to win their approval. He asked to take Rebekah back to Abraham's land so she could become the wife of Isaac.

Rebekah's family asked, "Will you go with this man?"

She replied, "I will go."

Thus, Rebekah became the first mail-order bride. She knew there were risks involved. These risks included never seeing her family because of the distance. She knew it was a long journey across treacherous and dangerous territory. She knew the risk in going a long way to marry a man she had never met. However, it was a marriage that had God's blessings. In the old *Book of Common Prayer*, there are these words in the marriage ceremony: "... as Isaac and Rebekah lived faithfully together, so may these persons surely perform the vows and covenants betwixt them made...."

As we look at Rebekah, it was clear she was a woman who knew life had its risks. Let us look at the risks that come our way in life.

I. The Risks Of Life Involve A Willingness To Reach For The Unknown

Down through the centuries, people have dared to reach for the unknown. There was the risk of conquering the seas; there was the risk of settling a new world; there was the risk to go into space and go where no one has gone before. There is always a risk when you dare to reach for the unknown. But the willingness to risk is what adds excitement to life. One person has said the oldest question in the world is a question of risk. That question is: "What's on the other side of the hill?"

Wherever you find men and women, you discover people asking this question. You discover men and women looking at the horizon of the unknown, attempting to conquer the unknown. The secrets of the unknown can tease and tantalize. There is no mountain so high and no wilderness so desolate that someone has not felt the urge to conquer it.

Sir Edmund Hilary, the first to climb Mount Everest, was asked, "Why climb it?" He replied, "Because it's there!"

John Glenn, the first American to orbit the earth, went back into space at the age of 77. A reporter asked, "Why do it at your age?" And he responded, "There are parts of the earth I never saw in the daylight. Besides, someone will do it; why not me?"

The risk of trying what has not been done before is what makes life exciting — even an adventure. The unknown always holds an adventure for us.

Thorwaldsen, the great artist, was asked, "What is your greatest statue?" He replied, "The next one." Chopin, the great music composer, would walk the floor, chewing on his quill pen and tearing up half-finished musical compositions. Why? Was it because he couldn't write music good enough to please people? No! It was because he couldn't write music good enough to please himself.

Jesus said that we must reach for perfection in our lives. He said, "Be ye perfect...." This is our goal. Of course, we never reach it! But we pursue it from one horizon to the next.

Today we are faced with some unknowns and they involve some risks. There are risks to our government in pursuing the truth, but we must believe it is only the truth which will set us free. There are risks to treating men and women with dignity and justice and equality — but we must be a people who are courageous enough to believe that no one is dispensable because every person is a child of God. There are risks to eliminating weapons of mass destruction from Iraq, but we cannot stand by idly while a cruel and evil regime develops methods to kill hundreds and thousands.

Our world is full of unknowns, but we must be willing to take the risks. After all, this is where each of us lives — on the fringes, looking into the unknown.

II. The Risks Of Life Involve An Assurance That God Is With You

In this Old Testament story, Rebekah was willing to take risks because she knew she was not alone. She resolved: "to inquire of the Lord." She knew that God's help was with her and the risks did not seem so frightening.

As we venture into the unknowns of life, we need to realize there is One who is with us. And that One is God. We may not be able to see him with our eyes, we may not be able to hear him with our ears, we may not be able to feel him with the touch of our hands ... but God is with us!

A man watches a boy holding a kite string. He looks up into the sky and the kite cannot be seen because it is so high. He asks, "Son, how do you know the kite is up there?"

"Because," the boy says, "I can feel the tug of the kite."

If you are ever tempted to doubt the reality that God is with you, simply be still for a moment and you will feel his tugging on the strings of your heart. William Carruth captured this idea in a poem:

> *Into our hearts high yearnings come*
> *Welling and surging in;*
> *Come from the mystic ocean*

Whose rim no foot has trod,
Some of us call it longing
And others call it God.

What is it that makes us willing to take all the risks of life? It is really no secret — it is God! Jesus called it the Kingdom God and he said: "The Kingdom of God is within you."

Whenever we venture into the unknown or dare to take certain risks in life, we plow ahead because we know that we are not alone — we know that God is with us. Across the centuries, no experience has challenged us to accept the risks and push back unknown frontiers except the sense of Someone greater than ourselves dwelling within us.

Do you believe that God is with you?

I know a young man, only 25 years of age, who seemed to have everything going his way. He had a good job that he enjoyed, he had a wife whom he loved very much, and he had an eighteen-month-old son named Christopher, Jr.

Then one morning, an act of violence changed all that. His wife worked in the Murrah Federal Building and she put the baby in the day care center in that building. Because of the warped minds of at least two men, Chris' wife and baby and 166 other people were killed.

One afternoon, while still trying to recover some of the trapped bodies in the rubble of the building, a police officer brought Chris to me. Chris had had the funeral for his wife and baby together. But now he wanted to put flowers on the bombsight.

I asked, "Do you have some flowers?"

"No!" he said. "I didn't think to bring any. I just wanted to come see the building and put some flowers on the site."

As I was explaining that if he brought back some flowers, we would carry them into the bombsight, one of the members of the Oklahoma City Council walked up carrying a heart-shaped bouquet of flowers with a small teddy bear in the middle. He was not aware of what we were talking about and asked, "Does anyone know what we should do with these flowers? Someone just gave them to me."

So, with Chris watching because he could not go into the area, some chaplains and I took the bouquet of flowers and placed them on the edge of the crater that had formed from the bomb blast. Afterward, I walked back to where Chris was standing. We talked for a little bit and I asked, "How are you doing?"

"It's hard," he said. "But, I'll make it. Someone gave me a little poem which helps."

Intrigued, I asked, "What poem?"

"I'm sure you've heard it before," he said. "I carry it in my pocket. It reminds me that I am not alone and that God is with me."

He reached into his pocket and pulled out a small card. It contained the words of a simple poem titled "Footprints in the Sand."

You are probably familiar with the poem by Katherine Simler. It concludes with these lines:

> "... I don't understand why in times when I needed you most, you should leave me."
> The Lord replied, "My precious, precious child, I love you and I would never leave you during your time of trial and suffering.
> When you saw only one set of footprints
> It was then that I carried you."

All of us needed to realize that Someone greater than ourselves is dwelling with us ... walking with us ... and sometimes, even carrying us through life. And when we understand this, the risk of life will seem less threatening ... less frightening ... less fearful ... because we know that God's love walks with us through all of life.

Prayer
O God, help us to know that we are never alone. Give us the courage to try great things in your name. Amen.

Chapter Four
Don't Look Back!

Genesis 19:26; 10:24-26

A woman came to see me. She was in her middle forties. She had been divorced for a couple of years. She indicated that all of her happiness in life ended when her marriage dissolved because her husband had left her for another woman. It was obvious from listening to her that she was not very happy with her life. As we talked, I asked her, "What has been exciting and interesting for you recently?"

Immediately, she began to list things from her past. She spoke of her wedding day, the birth of her children, and family vacations she used to go on.

I stopped her and said, "I am sure those were happy events and happy times, but they all happened in the past. What has been exciting in your life recently? What has made you happy recently?"

She was silent for a moment. Finally, she looked at me and said, "I guess nothing has made me happy recently."

This is a problem that many of us experience. We live in the past; we get our happiness from the past. We spend so much time living in the past that we miss the joy and excitement of living in the present. Of course, we want to hold on to the good things from our past — we want to remember happy times when we were younger — we don't ever want to let go of those special moments from our past. But, if we want to experience real happiness and joy in life, we need to be experiencing it now — today!

In other words, a basic mistake is to believe our joy and happiness in life are locked in our past. This is what Lot's wife believed. To be honest, we know very little about this woman of the Bible, because there isn't much information about her.

A youth group was trying to test their preacher. They asked some biblical questions, and then one asked what he thought was a difficult question. He asked, "What was the name of Lot's wife?"

I smiled. It was an easy question. I said, "Her name was 'Mrs. Lot.' "

The Bible does not list her name. In fact, only fifteen words in the Old Testament tell the story of Lot's wife. These fifteen words have placed her among the well-known women of the Bible. Those words are: "But, Lot's wife looked back (behind her) and was turned into a pillar of salt."

This is an odd and difficult story. Lot, with his wife and family, went to live in the city of Sodom. They built a home, began raising their family, and prospered while in Sodom.

One day some men came to Lot and warned him to get out of the city because it was going to be destroyed. Along with her husband, Lot's wife responded to the warning. She loved her home and wanted to remain in her home, but the threat of danger compelled her to leave. There was no enthusiasm in her leaving and she lingered. Safety was on the outskirts of the city, but she lingered. She did not want to leave Sodom; she did not want to leave her home. And as they were leaving the city, she turned for one more look. We then read she was turned into a pillar of salt.

What happened to her? Perhaps she lingered too long. Archaeologists believe there was pitch in the area and lightning ignited a fire and the pitch burned. Perhaps a strong wind pushed the flames and the city was destroyed. The woman could have been overtaken by flames and the sand of the desert, so she appeared frozen like a pillar of salt.

This is a difficult story because a literal interpretation indicates that God destroyed Sodom because of its wickedness. But we need to remember these people believed that whatever happened was caused by God. They believed that if a baby died, God caused it. If their country went to war and they won, God helped them to win and if they lost, God caused them to lose. They believed God caused everything and there was no cause and effect in life.

But God did not destroy the city, because God has never committed a sin. And God didn't turn that woman into a pillar of salt because God is not a god of vengeance. God is not a murderer. We have been introduced to Jesus and our idea of God is not as warped as it was before he came into this world and into our lives.

This story of Lot's wife is a powerful story. It is a story of a woman going in one direction but hearing a call in another. Life was calling to her from the hills and Sodom was calling to her with its memories. Today there are a few things which this story lifts up for our consideration.

I. Don't Look Back Because Things Have Changed

Lot's wife had all of her memories tied up in the city of Sodom. It was her home. It was where her friends were. It was where she had raised her children.

She longed to return. We can understand that! Nostalgia plays a major role in our lives. We long for the past because we are familiar with it and the future is always an unknown quality. But things change whether we like it or not. Life is like that; we cannot go back. Life is like a flowing stream. Put your hand in the stream, take it out and you can never go back to the same water, can you? The stream is in motion and so is life. It is constantly changing and we can never go back to the good old days.

Thomas Wolfe made this very clear in his autobiographical book, *You Can't Go Home Again*. In the book he deals with his own personal sorrow and deep disappointment. He weaves his story into the story of George Webber, a man who, early in life, succeeded beyond his fondest expectations. Like Alexander the Great, he conquered all that was known in his field while very young. But Webber soon learns the startling truth that fame and fortune do not offer the ultimate satisfaction.

So, he returned to his home in Asheville, North Carolina. He hoped to recapture some of the innocent joy of his youth. Traveling back, he dredged up old memories long stored and greatly embellished. He erased all the ugly and unpleasant memories. But the moment he stepped off the train, his dreams and rose-colored memories began to crumble beneath the weight of cruel reality. It had all changed! Then the truth began to dawn on him — the way back to yesterday is closed. There is one line which says: "He saw now that you can't go home again — not ever. There was no road back." Thomas Wolfe discovered a truth which is written into the fabric of life — the fact that none of us can go home again because things keep growing and changing.

Still, the desire is there and the Bible uses graphic language to teach us that you can't go home again. Lot's wife could not let go of the past and became a pillar of salt. The past hardens, the past atrophies, the past changes. The Bible, plainly and painfully, warns us not to look back because the past has changed. Satchel Page was more direct when he said: "Don't look back because they may be gaining on you."

II. Don't Look Back Because People Change

If you think that the change which came to Lot's wife was that she became a pillar of salt, then you have misunderstood the story. Her physical death was a mere accident as she lingered too long looking back at Sodom. Prior to entering Sodom, it is safe to assume that she shared the family faith. In all probability, she was a woman of faith and prayer. But once they entered Sodom, she allowed Sodom to enter her.

The change was slow, but gradually she was caught up in the life of the city and her faith began to lose its importance in her life. Her faith was replaced with a desire for material possessions, with a desire to climb the social ladder, with a desire for the temptations and passions which Sodom offered. As her faith was replaced with the desires of Sodom, she was changing as a person. On the way out of the city, she felt the pull of her faith and the pull of Sodom. She was torn between both. She was torn between two loves: she felt the lure of safety in the hills and she felt the pull of Sodom behind her and she realized that she was not the same. She had changed. And this change caused her to linger long enough so that death claimed her.

Whether we are willing to admit it or not, we all change. Life is an eloquent witness to the truth that you have changed. Just look in the mirror — you will see a face that has changed from twenty years ago.

An old preaching professor named William Stidger used to tell of his courtship with a young lady named Minnie Hood. As a young man he was madly in love with the beautiful Minnie Hood. But for some reason they never married. They went their separate ways and married other people. Then, some forty years later, Dr. Stidger and his wife were in Spokane, Washington, where Minnie Hood lived. After getting settled in their hotel, Dr. Stidger turned rather casually to his wife and asked, "Would you mind if we visited Minnie this evening?"

Mrs. Stidger had no objection. That evening they drove out to visit his old girlfriend from forty years before. When they reached her home, his heart was beating rapidly. For forty years he had carried around a mental picture of that beautiful girl he had once loved, and now he was about to see her again. The door was opened by a woman who weighed no less than 250 pounds. She had gray hair and wrinkles adorned her face. She looked so different that Dr. Stidger just stared and then stammered, "Minnie?"

After a pleasant visit with tea and cookies, Dr. and Mrs. Stidger left. As they were driving back to the hotel, she said, "Minnie looked terrible. I hardly recognized her."

His wife looked at him and asked, "William, did you ever stop to think what a shock your wrinkled old face and bald head must have been to Minnie?"

Everybody changes! You have changed and things are not the same. We may love that comfortable feeling of people being as we remember, but they never are! We all change!

The real question is, "What kind of changes do we allow to take places in our lives?" We may not be able to do much about the physical changes of ourselves, but we can do a lot about the changes that take place inside ourselves. We have an influence on our spiritual changes, our emotional changes, and our attitude on life. And that brings me to a final item from this story:

III. Don't Look Back ... Look Ahead To New Horizons

Lot's wife was moving toward safety, but she stopped and looked back. There was something in the past which commanded her attention and she paused, she looked back, and she died.

When the city of Pompeii was unearthed several days ago, the figure of a woman was found where the flow of lava had embalmed her. Her feet were pointed toward the city gate. Evidently, she was fleeing from the doom of that city.

Although her feet were pointed toward the city gate, her body was turned backward. Her hands were outstretched toward the ground. And just beyond her fingertips was a bag of pearls. Possibly she had dropped them. Perhaps they had been dropped by another. But it was apparent she was not looking to new horizons. She was looking to the past. The attitude of grasping greed had consumed her and as she turned to pick up the pearls, the lava overtook her and entombed her forever.

The challenge is for us to keep looking ahead at new horizons. There was a new horizon of hope for Lot's wife — but she chose to reject it.

God has put new horizons before you and me. And we have a choice! We can choose to turn back — but that would be a mistake. It would be a destructive choice. The other choice is not to look back. The other choice is to fix our eyes upon a new horizon; the other choice is to choose to walk with God each day of our lives. When you choose to walk with God, you are not looking backward; you are not lingering in a forgotten past. You are choosing to face a world that is jammed full, a world that is pregnant with new horizons — a world that is overflowing with new possibilities.

An old gospel song concludes with these words: "I don't know what the future holds, but I know Who holds the future." So, I challenge you to make a decision about your future. I challenge you to choose this day Whom you will serve. I challenge you — *don't look back!* Instead, look at the new horizon of possibilities that God has given you in Jesus Christ.

Prayer

O God, we give thanks for the love of Jesus Christ which is always with us and always challenging us to live and walk with him. In his name, we pray. Amen.

Chapter Five
A Mixed-Up Story

Genesis 29:15-30

It was Christmas Day and our family had opened all the presents. We were talking and enjoying being together, waiting to eat Christmas dinner. I took some time to run over to the hospital and visit someone who was spending Christmas Day in the hospital.

When I got on the elevator to leave, a couple of women were already there. One lady kept staring at me. Finally she asked, "Are you that preacher on television? You were on television last night."

We had televised our Christmas Eve services the night before and I was flattered she had watched our services. I said, "Yes, ma'am! Our services were on television last night."

"I thought I recognized you," she said. "Since my husband has been ill, we get our church from television."

She proceeded to tell me *all* about her husband's illness. Then she suddenly remembered she had not introduced me to her husband's sister, the lady with her on the elevator. So she said to her sister-in-law, "This is the preacher we watch on television sometimes. This is Dr. Robert Jeffress."

Talk about the wind going out of your sails! I didn't think I even looked Baptist! The woman on the elevator had me mixed up — she had me confused with someone else.

The story of Leah and Rachel is also confused and mixed up. The Old Testament writer had an eye for the dramatic when he introduced this story with its plots, subplots, and innuendoes. Yet Leah and Rachel are important women because they became the wives of Jacob and the mothers of twelve children — whom we know as the Twelve Tribes of Israel.

The Old Testament stories are often told from the standpoint of the hero, and he is a clever, charming, deceitful, manipulative, and charismatic individual. Jacob had connived to get his brother's birthright, but once he had it, he became frightened. He was afraid his brother Esau would kill him. Jacob had gotten what he wanted, but he had to flee his home because he had wronged his brother.

Jacob decided to go to his mother's homeland, Ur of the Chaldees. He would stay with his uncle. He made the 500-mile journey on foot. He must have been weary from the trip and scorched by the sun. When he arrived he asked some shepherds about Laban, his mother's brother. They said: "Behold, Rachel, his daughter comes with the sheep."

Jacob saw a bright-eyed, beautiful maiden, in a brilliantly colored dress. He fell in love at first sight with Rachel and wanted to marry her. Laban was a man who knew how to drive a bargain. He said, "Work for me seven years and you can marry her."

The seven years passed as if they were but "a few days." Then, when it came time for the marriage, there was a mix-up ... there was confusion ... there were some complications.

Laban pulled a switch at the wedding festivities. The switch was easy to do because in those primitive times, it was the custom to conduct the bride to the bedchamber of her husband in silence and darkness. It wasn't until the next morning that Jacob discovered the switch. He discovered the girl he had married was not Rachel, but Rachel's older sister, Leah.

Of course, Jacob complained to Laban. Laban only said, "It is unthinkable that I would allow the younger daughter to be married first. Work seven more years for me and you can marry Rachel." So, one week after marrying Leah, Jacob married Rachel and then worked for Laban seven more years.

Yes, the story of Leah and Rachel is a mixed-up and confusing story. Laban had manipulated and tricked Jacob into marrying both of his daughters. And it is easy to imagine the problems which arose in this polygamist household where two sisters were married to the same man. If there ever was a story that was confusing and mixed up, it is this story of Leah and Rachel and their marriage to Jacob.

This morning, I want to look at some elements of this mixed-up story and see how they apply to us.

I. The Story of Leah And Rachel Is A Story of Love

From the moment that Jacob saw Rachel with her father's sheep, he fell in love. He loved her so much he was willing to serve as an indentured servant for fourteen years. Jacob's love for Rachel is part of the fabric of this story.

There is something within us that identifies with the love that Rachel and Jacob shared. Perhaps it is simply that we long to be loved; we want to know if we are loved by another. Something within us yearns to know if we are loved.

One of my favorite plays is *Fiddler On The Roof*. In one scene, Tevye comes into his house and watches his wife working in the kitchen. Finally, he gets the courage to ask a question that has been on his mind. He asks: "Golda, do you love me?"

Regardless of who we are in this world — regardless of position or power in life — we all have the desire to love and be loved by others. And we all want confirmation of love. We want to *know* if we are loved.

But, as everyone discovers, the love between individuals can be very fragile. Sometimes things simply go wrong in a relationship. Sometimes there is betrayal, cheating, and heartache and things simply do not work out as we planned.

In the biblical story we read earlier, Rachel knew she was loved by Jacob. His love for her didn't end because he was cheated. He did not strike out in anger because Laban pulled a fast one. He just kept working to win the hand of the one he loved.

And this is what God does with us as we make our journey through life. We may be crafty individuals and conniving individuals who seek to take advantage of others. We may have lives filled with sin. We may make God so angry that he is tempted to abandon us. But God will not abandon us nor can his love for us be destroyed. God continues working and loving us because of Jesus Christ.

II. The Story Of Leah And Rachel Is Also A Story Of Rejection

Put yourself in Leah's position for a moment. Leah was not unattractive. It was simply that her younger sister was "beautiful." Leah was married to Jacob and had several children by him. But she knew she was not loved by Jacob. How often do you suppose she was aware that Jacob preferred to be with her sister Rachel?

Leah was a human being and she was hurt by the knowledge that her husband preferred to be with another. Her heart ached at being rejected. Even when she was with him, she knew she was being rejected. As a matter of fact, it is very difficult to feel rejection if you are *not* with somebody. If you are far away, you may be unaware that someone is rejecting you. However, if someone is close, you sense or feel the rejection.

Rejection happens in a variety of ways. As we grow older, we experience rejection. Blacks have been rejected because of the color of their skin. Jews have been rejected because of their religion. College students have been rejected from sororities or fraternities because they didn't fit the special mold. Women have been rejected for jobs they were qualified for simply because they were women. White males have been rejected for jobs because affirmative action laws required a company to choose another.

We have all experienced rejection at one time or another. The hurt is real and the scars are still visible in our lives. The challenge facing us is not to allow the rejection to control our lives.

One afternoon several years ago, I received a phone call from a medical doctor in my church. I tried to begin a pleasant conversation with him, but he was very direct and said, "Robert, can you come to my office, right now?"

From the sound of his voice, I knew something was not right. "Doc," I asked, "what's wrong?"

"I have a young man with a gun in my office," he said. "He's threatening to kill himself. Now he wants to talk to a minister, so I called you."

I remember thinking about saying, "Thanks a lot, Doc." But instead, I said, "I'll be right over!"

When I got there, an ambulance was waiting and police cars surrounded the building. I told them who I was and walked into the office. The doctor, one of his nurses, and the young man with the gun were in the reception area. I am sure I didn't follow procedures. I simply introduced myself as a Methodist minister and suggested it would be better if the doctor and nurse left so he and I could talk privately. He allowed the nurse to leave, but wanted the doctor to stay.

He told me his name and I asked, "Jim, what's going on? Why have you been holding these people and threatening to kill yourself?"

He spoke about problems at work and some other things. Finally, he got around to the details of his life. While growing up he had difficulties with his stepfather. He struggled in school and frequently got into fights and ended up in a juvenile center. Still, he seemed to be turning his life around until that October afternoon when his fiancée announced she was breaking off their relationship.

Then the young man with the gun looked at me and said, "Nobody gives a darn about me."

"Jim, that's not true," I said. "The Doc here cares about you or he wouldn't have wasted his time with you. I care about you or I wouldn't have come in to talk with you. And, even more important, God cares about you. He promises to help you deal with the hurt and heartaches and rejections in life."

We talked a little more and I asked, "Can we pray together?"

"That would be good," he said.

"Hand the gun to the doctor," I said, "so I can hold your hands while we pray." And he did! There in the reception room of a doctor's office, I prayed for a young man who had been rejected so much that the pain and heartache almost overwhelmed him. But now, with God's help, he was choosing to remember that there was One who loved him and would help him whenever he felt alone and rejected.

You, too, may have experienced rejection in your life. The pain is real ... the heartache is real ... and the promise of God's love is real.

III. The Story Of Leah And Rachel Is A Story Of Relationships

You have heard the old saying, "Three's a crowd." I am sure there was jealousy and bickering between those two sisters married to the same man. But there came the day that Jacob asked their help to return to the land of his birth. For the first time, Rachel and

Leah were united in their desire to help Jacob. They pulled together because of their love for Jacob and in the process built a relationship that made them stronger and more supportive of each other.

I know a man who owned a business that failed. Everything he had worked for was lost. To make matters even worse, he had no money to help his son through college. His son would have to work his way through school.

As they said their good-byes at the airport, the father said, "Son, I'm sorry! I wanted you to have it easy while you were in school, so you could concentrate on your studies."

The son looked at the father and said, "Dad, you gave me what I needed most. You gave me your love and I *will* make it!"

When your relationship is right, you are stronger than you think you are. You will discover an inner strength to help you weather any storm. You will discover a backbone you didn't realize you had.

The writers of the Bible seemed to understand this. When someone felt alone and under pressure, we hear the promise of God over and over again: "Lo, I am with you always."

Do you know what this promise is?

It is God promising you the strength to face anything that comes your way in life. It is God promising you his love each and every day of your life. It is God promising you a relationship with his Son, Jesus Christ.

Have you accepted this promise for your life?

Prayer

O God, for your presence in our lives through Jesus Christ, help us to be thankful. In his name. Amen.

Chapter Six
Letters In The Sand
John 8:1-11

One year my wife and I had the opportunity to take a vacation to the tropical paradise of Cancun, Mexico. We enjoyed the trip with some sailing on the sea, snorkeling in the crystal clear water near the barrier reef, and a bus trip inland to see the ruins of Chichen Itza. It was a great trip which we thoroughly enjoyed.

One morning, while we were lounging around on the beach under those little grass cabanas, reading a book or snoozing in the beach-recliner, I saw a young man carrying a stick. Every few feet or so, he would draw a square in the sand. He would write something in the sand and then he walked down a few feet and repeated the process all over again.

As you might imagine, curiosity got the better of me and I got up and strolled over to see what he was writing in the sand. As I read his message I couldn't help but smile. The writings reminded me of the old Burma Shave signs which used to be along the highways. The messages the young man had written in the sand were: "Dear Ann ... If you follow these letters ... written in the sand ... you will find a man ... who wants to put a ring on your hand ... Love, Dan."

I don't know if his unique way of proposing marriage was successful, but it certainly attracted the attention of those who strolled by on the beach and saw the letters in the sand.

The only record we have of Jesus ever writing anything is the letters in the sand that he wrote one day. But the winds of time have long since erased those tracings in the sand. However, the story remains and it is considered to be one of the most powerful stories about Jesus.

In the story, the Pharisees brought a woman caught in the act of adultery and threw her at the feet of Jesus. We do not know the name of the woman. She is simply a nameless woman the Pharisees had caught in a single act, and they were using her in a plan to trap Jesus.

The woman lies before Jesus, sobbing and trembling in shame — shame for her sinful act and shame because she was not fully clothed after being caught in the act of adultery. What clothing she has, she wraps about her body as the Pharisees spew out accusations. In heated voices they shout out the vile names reserved for such women. Then, one Pharisee with a sly grin on his face looks at Jesus and says, "This woman has been caught in the act of adultery. What should happen to her?"

Jesus understood the situation immediately. They have not brought her to him for judgment. They have already judged her guilt. They have brought her to Jesus to entrap him. It is a clever scheme. If Jesus says the woman should be set free, he will have repudiated the law of Moses. If he says the woman should be stoned as the law of Moses authorized, Jesus would be in direct conflict with the Roman authorities, because in their laws they were the only ones with the power of life and death.

Yes, it was a clever trap. Either way, the Pharisees would be able to discredit Jesus. So, they press the question — "Jesus, what do you say should happen to this woman?"

Jesus does not look at the woman. Instead, he looks into the face of each man in the crowd. He sees the rocks in their hands and the hatred in their eyes. Everyone was waiting for his answer. The sounds in the courtyard have died out. The merchants are no longer hawking their wares. The only sound to be heard is the quiet sobs of the woman trembling at his feet. Jesus bends down and begins writing some letters in the sand. The Pharisees are persistent, as they demand of Jesus, "What will you do with the woman caught in the act of adultery?"

Finally, Jesus looks up into the faces of the men and, with eyes which never blink, he says: "He that is without sin among you, let him cast the first stone." In that one short sentence, he went to the heart of the matter. I am sure the look of smug self-righteousness drained from their faces. Suddenly, they realize they, too, are being judged. And they watch as Jesus continues writing his letters in the sand.

What did Jesus write that day in the sand? No one knows for sure. Some theologians believe he wrote words describing the Pharisees. They say he wrote *liar*, and in the silence a stone dropped to the ground and one man slipped away. Next, he wrote *drunkard*, and another dropped his stone and walked away in shame. He wrote the words *thief* ... *adulterer* ... *murderer* ... and as each word is traced in the sand, more stones dropped with a thud to the ground. One by one the Pharisees slipped away in shame. They had come to judge the woman, but the letters in the sand had judged them.

This story of the nameless woman taken in the very act of adultery is a powerful story. It is a story which makes clear how far a loving God is willing to go in his love for us — even when we choose to walk on the dark side. Today, I want to lift up some ideas we need to remember.

I. Jesus Refused To Condemn The Nameless Woman

There is no doubt that the woman deserved to be condemned. She had violated one of the commandments and was caught in the act of adultery. I've always wondered where the man was. Although the Mosaic law demands the same punishment for the man, men in that time held a superior and privileged position. Therefore, the man involved was not brought forward for punishment.

To the Pharisees, the woman deserved to be condemned. She was guilty and the law was clear. But Jesus saw the nameless woman in a different light. He did not see her as a worthless sinner in need of condemnation, but as a child of God.

There are so many opportunities in our world today to condemn someone who has done something wrong. Alcohol or drugs became a problem in someone's life and we are ready to condemn him. A marriage breaks up and we hear a third person is the cause and we are ready to cast our stones. We see people who are struggling with temptations we label as sin and we are ready to brand them as sinners, and condemn them to a hell that is beyond God's love.

But Jesus, when he was confronted with a sinner who deserved condemnation, refused to condemn. Perhaps the lesson we need to learn from this is we should be slow to condemn, we should be slow to be judgmental, we should be slow to cast stones. Perhaps we need to follow the example of Jesus and remember that every person is a child of God.

Billy Graham appeared on the Larry King show on CNN. Billy Graham is one of the most respected religious leaders in the world. They talked about a variety of subjects. They spoke about Graham's health and his Parkinson's disease. They spoke about the number of crusades he still does each year. They spoke about his son, Franklin, picking up the load and preaching at some of the crusades for him. They spoke about the execution of Karla Kaye Tucker.

Then Larry King turned the subject to politics. He said, "I understand you are a friend of President and Mrs. Clinton."

"Yes," Billy responded. "I have been fortunate to be a friend of every President since Eisenhower."

"Well," Larry King said, "you know the charges about the President and the intern, Monica Lewinsky. How do you feel about that?"

Billy Graham was quiet for a moment, then he said, "As you know, the key word is 'alleged.' We don't know if the charges are true or not. However, if they are, I would be disappointed."

Isn't that an interesting response? He reminded us that a person is innocent until proven guilty. However, if a person is guilty, Billy Graham was not going to condemn, he was not going to throw stones; he simply said he would be disappointed. If we are to follow the footsteps of Jesus, perhaps we need to drop the stones. Perhaps we need to refrain from condemning others. Perhaps we need to remember that everyone — including sinners — is a child of God.

II. Jesus Was Willing To Forgive The Nameless Woman

The Pharisees dropped their stones and slipped away. The woman was left alone with Jesus. He stopped writing letters in the sand and looked at the woman lying before him on the ground. He asked her: "Woman, where are your accusers? Has no one condemned you?" The woman looked up for the first time and replied, "No one, Lord." This is the only thing the woman says in this story. She did not attempt to justify herself or explain what happened. She simply replied with relief in her voice, "No one, Lord." Then,

Jesus rendered his verdict. He said, "Neither do I condemn you. Go and sin no more."

This is a strange response from Jesus. Jesus did not wink at her sin, nor does he excuse it with an easy alibi. He did not accuse her of guilt, nor did he absolve her from blame. He did not condone her act. He simply told her, "Go and sin no more." Her act of adultery was a sin. It was a violation of the Ten Commandments. It was a violation of her marriage vows. She was guilty and deserved punishment. But Jesus forgave her.

This is the greatest miracle of all — God's willingness to forgive us of our sins. And it should be something we learn to put into practice. If we want to walk in the footsteps of Jesus, we need to be willing to forgive. God needs people like you and me to be willing to forgive even when forgiveness is not warranted.

Do you remember Johan Bojer's story titled *The Great Hunger*? The principal character was Peer Holm, a famous engineer. He built bridges to span great rivers, built railroads across desolate deserts, and dug tunnels through majestic mountains. He had a farm in a small village.

If you remember the story, you know that he lived beside a neighbor who had a vicious dog. Peer Holm was afraid for his little girl and asked the man to keep his dog penned or chained up. However, the owner of the dog ignored the request. One day, Peer Holm was walking across his field when he heard the screams of his little girl. He ran in the direction of the screams and saw the dog at the throat of his daughter. He tore the vicious animal away but it was too late. The life was gone from her body.

The entire village was upset with the owner of the dog. He had been warned but he had ignored their advice. So, the people of the village decided to shun the man. They ostracized him. They refused to do business with him. In the spring when he plowed his field no one would sell him seed to plant. His field was left bare and he was left isolated and hated by the people of the village.

One moonlit night, Peer Holm, the father of the little girl, could no longer stand the hatred. There in the moonlight he took half of his own seed and went into the field of his neighbor. However, you can't keep something like that a secret for very long and later in the spring, the villagers noticed an empty section in Peer Holm's field and grain growing in the neighbor's field. They saw forgiveness of the sin.

Forgiveness is something God offers to us — in spite of our sins. Like the woman thrown at the feet of Jesus, we too are guilty of sin. We too are deserving of condemnation. We too know there is no reason we should expect any leniency. But then come those dramatic and powerful words of Jesus: "Neither do I condemn you. Go and sin no more."

What else do you need to hear? Just as Jesus gave that nameless woman of long ago another chance, he stands ready to give you another chance. He stands ready to forgive you. He stands ready to keep on loving you because you are a child of God.

I doubt there is another story in the Bible which more powerfully proclaims God's love and willingness to forgive than this story where Jesus said: "Neither do I condemn you. Go and sin no more."

Prayer

O God, help us to know that your love and forgiveness is available to us because of your redeeming grace. In Jesus' name. Amen.

Chapter Seven
Be All That You Can Be

Luke 7:36-50

We were out in the hallway waiting for the wedding to begin. Like most grooms, he was nervous. He paced up and down the hallway as the minutes ticked away.

He was a Private First Class in the U.S. Army. I knew he was stationed at Fort Bragg, North Carolina. So, to help calm down this young soldier right before his wedding, we began to talk about Fort Bragg. I have an aunt who lives in Fayetteville, North Carolina, where Fort Bragg is located and I have been on that base several times. I asked him if he was in the Airborne Division.

"Yes, sir!" he replied. "I'm in the 101st Airborne. They are the best."

You could hear the pride in his voice and you could see the pride on his face as he talked about his division. You could tell he was proud to be serving his country.

As we continued to talk, I asked him, "What influenced you to join the Army?"

"Well," he said, "there were many factors. Joining the Army was a way to help support my mother and it was a way to build up credit to help pay for my college education. But I suppose the real reason was their promise."

"What promise is that?" I asked.

"You know," he said. "The promise in their advertising, to help me be all that I can be."

The Scripture passage in Luke tells one of the most beautiful and appealing stories in the Gospels. Jesus was dining in the courtyard of Simon the Pharisee. Scarcely had the meal begun when a woman came and stood at the feet of Jesus.

The Bible does not gloss over the situation. The Bible describes the woman as a "sinner." She sold herself in the streets to satisfy the sensual desires of men. And now, she had walked into Simon's courtyard and stood at the feet of Jesus.

Access to Simon's house was easy. The rules of hospitality were surprisingly free. Uninvited guests were welcome to come in and sit along the walls and listen to the conversations of a distinguished teacher. Most likely, there were several uninvited guests who had come to listen to Jesus.

However, the appearance of this particular woman caused some murmuring among the people. It was scandalous that she should even be present. Simon was embarrassed that she had intruded into his dinner party. Simon was shocked that Jesus did not order her to leave at once when she began to anoint his feet with an expensive ointment. But Jesus looked at this woman in a different way. Jesus saw more than a woman who peddled her flesh in the street; Jesus saw more than a woman who was an outcast and a sinner. Jesus saw a woman who was changing. Jesus saw a woman who was living in the depths of sin, but now she was trying to change and become all that she could be. Jesus saw the possibility for good that was deep inside this woman if she would only realize what she could be.

The Good News of the gospel is that there is a possibility for good buried deep inside each of us. We may do what we know to be wrong ... we may do those things which fill us with shame ... we may have walked the path of sin for so long that guilt overwhelms us. But the clear message of this dramatic story from the Bible is that we still have the possibility of change and of becoming all that God calls us to be.

Today, I want to lift up some ideas from this story and discuss how you and I can become all that we can be, looking closely at how we can live out the possibility that is within each of us.

I. You Become All That You Can Be When You Realize That You Are Not Self-Sufficient

There is a difference between Simon and the woman. Simon is not a villain. He is curious about Jesus and invites him to his home. But Simon is unwilling to get very close to Jesus. The severest indictment we can bring against Simon is that he is not conscious of any real need in his life. Simon thinks he has his life in order and cannot see the possibility of being any better than he is. Simon believes he is self-sufficient and does not have a real need to be closer to Jesus.

Too many of us are like Simon. Our minds are closed to any real problems in life. We have a tendency to believe we are self-sufficient and do not have any need for God in our lives.

I recently visited the new office suites of a church member. He is the senior partner of a law firm of fifty attorneys. I noticed on a shelf in his new office a Navy bell, a few medals, and a Bible with a hole through it.

He saw me looking at the Bible and told me a story from World War II. He was a young Navy officer, a Lt. Commander who had not grown up in the church. He had never really thought very much about God. On the day they were getting ready for the invasion of Okinawa, the chaplain came by and gave him a Bible. He was busy, so he stuck it in his shirt pocket.

About twenty minutes later, the bell for "battle stations" sounded. A flight of Kamikaze planes began attacking the naval task force. Suddenly, something slammed into his chest and knocked him flat on his back. He had trouble breathing because of the impact of the shrapnel that had hit him. He grabbed his chest and was surprised there was no blood. The shrapnel had torn into the Bible in his pocket and had stopped on the passage in 2 Corinthians 12:9 which says: "My grace is sufficient for you...."

Far too often, we go about living our lives thinking we can make it on our own, thinking we have no need for God's help or help from anyone else, thinking we are entirely self-sufficient in the living of our lives. But the simple truth is that we can never be everything we are meant to be — everything we are called to be — until we see a need for God in our lives.

·But the Good News is that God's grace is sufficient.

II. You Become All That You Can Be When You Realize That Love Is The Most Powerful Force On Earth

The woman in the story is a notoriously bad woman. She is widely known as a prostitute and is shunned by the respectable people of the community. However, when and where she came in contact with Jesus, we do not know. Perhaps she had stood at the edge of a crowd and had listened to him speak. And as she listened to Jesus speak, she felt his words of love go directly into her heart. As she listened to him speak, she suddenly felt the weight of her sins being lifted. As she listened to him speak, she realized that his love could give her a new life — a life filled with new hope and new possibilities.

So the night she sought out Jesus to express her gratitude for the cleansing power of his love. She had a new sense of dignity, of worth, and purity as a person. So she sought out Jesus at Simon's house. Around her neck she wore a costly phial of perfume. She began to anoint his feet with the perfume and, as she did so, she became so overwhelmed with emotion that she wept. Love is a powerful emotion that can bring a new hope, a new sense of self-worth, and a new desire to be all that we can be.

Roy Smith grew up on the plains of Kansas. His father worked as a mill hand and never made a lot of money. But his father wanted him to go to the small Methodist college in their town. Somewhere in the back of his mind, Roy knew it was a sacrifice for his parents to put him through college, but he rarely thought about it. He was enjoying school too much to worry about the expense.

When Roy made the debate team, he mentioned how nice it would be to have a new suit and new shoes for an upcoming event. Somehow, his parents managed to buy the new suit and new shoes for their son.

Then just before the debate was to begin, someone burst through the doors of the auditorium and told Roy that his father had been badly hurt in an accident at the mill. Roy ran down the streets of the little town to the mill, but it was too late. His father had died.

They buried him on a cold and windy day. After the funeral, Roy went over to the mill to pick up some of his father's belongings. Someone had thoughtfully put them into a cardboard box. When Roy looked into the box, his father's old work shoes were lying on top with the bottoms up. Those shoes had holes that stretched from side to side. He then realized that while he wore new shoes to a debate, his father had stood on the cold steel floor of the grain mill in shoes that did not protect his feet. In that instance, Roy Smith knew the sacrifice and love his father had made for him. In that moment, as the tears streamed down his face, Roy Smith sensed a new determination to go on with his college education and become all that he could be.

Yes, love is the most powerful force on earth. When you realize the love that God has for you — you begin to catch a glimpse of all that you can be.

III. You Become All That You Can Be When You Realize That You Are Forgiven

The woman's sin was not condoned; it was forgiven. Jesus made her feel that she could rise above her evil past and her sinful present. He simply looked at her and said: "Your sins are forgiven."

This is the hope that we all have. Deep within our lives some sin may lie buried. But the redeeming hope of the gospel is that we can be forgiven. The sins of our lives can be pardoned and we get a fresh start ... another chance ... a new beginning ... an opportunity to become all that God wants us to be.

Dr. A. J. Cronin tells of a young nurse in charge of a little boy who was desperately ill with diphtheria. His throat was choked with membrane and he had only a slender chance to live. A tube was inserted into his throat to help him breathe.

The nurse was stationed by the bed to keep the tube cleared. But she fell asleep and awakened to find the tube blocked. Instead of following the instructions and clearing the membranes, a simple matter of routine nursing, she lost her head and bolted in panic. Hysterically she called the doctor out of his sleep, but when he arrived the child was dead.

He was angry that a child should die so needlessly by blundering negligence. That very night he sat down and wrote a report to the Health Board and demanded that the nurse be dismissed. He then called the nurse in and with a voice trembling with resentment he read his report to her.

The young nurse stood there in silence — shame and guilt on her face and tears in her eyes. Finally the nurse looked at the doctor and with a stammering plea, she said, "Give me ... give me another chance."

The doctor was surprised. Certainly, he had not considered that. It was a breach of discipline and there was nothing to do but to punish her. He dismissed her, sealed his report, and went back to bed.

But he could not sleep because words kept whispering in his mind: "Forgive us our trespasses, as we forgive those who trespass against us ..." The next morning he got up and tore up his report. And this young nurse went on to become the head of a large hospital and one of the most respected nurses in Great Britain. Why? Because she was pardoned! Because she was given another chance! Because she was forgiven!

This is the theme the New Testament shouts from Matthew to Revelation — there is forgiveness with God. You may have walked the path of sin ... you may be overwhelmed with shame and guilt because of those sins ... you may be embarrassed with the way you have been living your life. But you can be forgiven! You can be all that you can be. You, too, can hear Jesus say to you as he did that woman at Simon's house: "Your sins are forgiven."

Prayer

O God, help us to accept the forgiveness you offer to us in Jesus Christ. In his name. Amen.

Chapter Eight
Great Things In Unexpected Moments

John 4:5-30

It was January 1991. All the news reports indicated we would soon be at war with Iraq. In fact, President Bush had given Sadaam Hussein until January 15 to withdraw from Kuwait or face war with the United States and a host of other nations.

I was attending a banquet where I had been asked to sit at the head table and give the invocation. The special speaker for the evening was Admiral William Crowell, the former chairman of the Joint Chiefs of Staff, the highest-ranking person in our military for several years in the Reagan and Bush administrations.

During dinner, we talked about the prospect of war with Iraq. Admiral Crowell was prophetic as he said, "If Sadaam Hussein refuses to withdraw from Kuwait, he will be making a mistake. I know the capability of his military and it is no match for ours. General Schwarzkopf will roll over him so efficiently and so quickly that the Iraqui military will be devastated."

Other people sitting at the table asked the Admiral some other questions. He did not dodge any question nor did he seem condescending. It was obvious he was proud of the men and women who serve in our military, and proud of the role he played in rebuilding our military during his tenure as Chair of the Joint Chiefs of Staff. And he was confident of what our military was capable of doing, if called upon to use force.

Then someone asked, "Admiral, do you see anything 'good' coming from the confrontation?"

The Admiral thought about the question for a few minutes. Then he said: "Great things have a way of coming about in an unexpected moments. Two years ago, no one was predicting the fall of communism ... the breakup of the Soviet Union ... the uniting of the two Germanys ... or that Russia and the USA would be cooperating in the dismantling of our nuclear missile systems. But unexpected moments do come in life and when they do, great things begin to happen."

This is what happened to the woman of Samaria. The noonday sun beat down on her as she made her way toward the well. Her face, once pretty and happy, was now hard and sad. Her figure, once beautiful and voluptuous, was now showing signs of age. And she made her way to the well in the heat of the day because she wanted to avoid the gossipy women who came in the cool of the morning. Her loose way of living made her a prime target of their gossip. The whispering behind her back, the stinging darts of sarcasm, the names they would call out to her face were enough to compel her to go to the well at noontime.

At the well she had an unexpected encounter with Jesus. The hatred which existed between the Jews and the Samaritans was almost 400 years old and centered around the location of the temple. The Jews had their temple in Jerusalem, while the Samaritans had their rival temple built on Mount Gerizim in the center of Samaria.

When she got to the well, Jesus said, "Give me a drink."

The request came as a surprise to the woman. It was not customary for a man to speak to a woman in public, and it was more unusual for a Jew to speak to a Samaritan. She was stunned at the encounter and she had no comprehension of how this brief encounter would change her life. Isn't this the way life is arranged? Some unexpected moments may continue to have a significant effect for a long time. You never know when some great things will swivel on those unexpected moments.

A young French doctor sat in a Paris park one day and watched some children playing a game with an old discarded plank. One boy would tap the plank with a pebble and the other boy, with his ear on the plank, would decipher the message. That unexpected moment caused the doctor to start thinking. Soon he developed the stethoscope.

Hank Ketchum, a cartoonist, came home from work one evening and found his wife in tears. "Hank!" she said, "our son Dennis is a menace!" That did it! An unexpected moment and a great idea began to take shape.

In California during the summer of 1872, it was so hot the grapes were shriveling on the vine. One farmer sent his crop of dried-up grapes to a grocer in San Francisco and asked him to sell them. The grocer, with a little imagination, sold them as "Peruvian Delicacies" and Sun-Maid raisins were on their way.

A swaggering English nobleman put a piece of meat between two pieces of bread. That is not much when you think about it, but "sandwich," named after the Earl of Sandwich, has become a household word and a way of life for most people at lunch.

The woman at the well had no idea what was in store for her that day she encountered Jesus. But that is the fascinating thing about life and the way in which seemingly insignificant events lead to important results. If there is one thing we should know about life, it is that great things often come in unexpected moments. Today we will look at some great things which happened to this woman because of her unexpected encounter with Jesus of Nazareth.

I. One Great Thing From An Unexpected Moment Is A New Direction In Life

The woman who encountered Jesus at the well in Samaria came to the well with a heart aching from her immoral past. She was an outcast in her own village, ostracized by the women, and used as a trollop by the men. But the day she encountered Jesus was a great day in her life. It was great because those few unexpected moments with Jesus gave her a new direction in life.

When reading the Scripture (John 4:5-30), you realize that Jesus confronted her about the brokenness in her personal life. She was bewildered that he knew so much about her, and when she went back to the village, she told them, "Come and see a man who knows all about me."

However, the change of direction in her life did not come about simply because Jesus confronted her with her immorality. Everyone in the village knew about her immoral behavior and gossiped about her affairs.

The great thing which influenced her and gave her a new direction to her life was the fact that he knew all about her and saw her as someone of value. In spite of the sins of her life, he still offered her "living water." She ran back to the village and said to everyone who would listen. "Come and see a man who knows all about me and he still loves me."

A few years ago, I was talking to a couple who had come to me to get married. He was a detective on the police force in another city and she worked at a local college. Usually, when I counsel a couple about their upcoming marriage, I ask a few questions. This is not to be nosey, but questions help me get to know the couple a little better. So I looked at this couple and asked, "How did you two meet?"

Most of the time when I ask this question, I get responses like: "We met in high school or college." "We met on the elevator at work." "We met at a party." "A friend introduced us."

However, when I asked this couple "How did you meet?" there was complete silence. It was as if I had asked the most embarrassing question imaginable. The silence was overwhelming. Finally, after they exchanged several glances with one another, they both smiled. The young police detective looked at me and said, "We met when I arrested her."

Somewhat surprised, I said, "You arrested her?"

"Yes," the officer said. "I was doing undercover work in some bars and she tried to sell me a $100 drink."

Now, you and I both know what he meant.

The girl, who had been silent, now said, "That was two years ago and my life was a mess. But Tom helped me get a decent job. He helped me to see my own worth as an individual and he helped me to understand that I could change. I guess that is why I love him so much. He knows all about me and he still loves me."

The great thing about unexpected moments is a quality of importance, of significance, of value, and of richness which can come out of common and ordinary events of life. Life is so arranged that what happens in an unexpected moment may be so monumental that it may go on having significance for a long time.

In other words, you never know when some great thing will come out of a common and ordinary event that gives a new direction to life. Great things often swivel on the unexpected moment. Do you realize the power that is available to help shape and direct your life in moments like this?

II. Another Great Things From Unexpected Moments Is The Opportunity To Share Our Understanding Of God

I doubt very seriously if the woman of Samaria started out toward the well within the intention of having a theological debate. It was simply when she saw a Jew at Jacob's well, she could not resist the satirical remark: "I see you are a prophet, sir. My Samaritan ancestors worshiped God on this mountain, but you Jews say that Jerusalem is the place where we should worship God." She was not interested in a theological debate. She was simply using this unexpected encounter to fan the flames of a religious controversy still smoldering after 400 years.

But Jesus used these unexpected moments to proclaim a new understanding of God. She had only wanted to inflame his anger, but Jesus declared to her two tremendous truths. First he said: "God is Spirit and they that worship him must worship in Spirit and in truth." He had only asked her for water in the beginning, but he gently used this unexpected opportunity to teach her a profound new truth: "God is Spirit."

The second new understanding of God that Jesus declared to this nameless woman of Samaria was that he was the Messiah, he was God's anointed one, he was the Christ — and because she received this message, she has an immortal place in the Bible.

We all have those opportunities to share our understanding of God. We all have those unexpected moments when the casual conversation suddenly turns profound and we have the opportunity to share our faith.

Once, as I walked into a Catholic hospital, the Sister in the Pastoral Care office asked me if I would go by and see a man. He had cancer and had asked to talk with a Methodist minister.

When I entered the room and introduced myself, "John" cut right through the generalities. He told me he had not been much of a Christian, although he had gone to a Methodist Sunday school when he was a boy. But church had not meant much in his life.

However, when the doctor told him he did not have long to live, he wanted to ask some questions. Then he paused for a moment as though he was struggling to put into words a painful thought. As I watched him, tears rolled down his cheeks, and finally he asked, "What's it like to die?"

I looked at this man, emaciated from the cancer, and asked, "Do you have any children?"

"Yes," he replied. "I have two sons. One lives in Houston and the other lives in Dallas."

"Do you remember when your children were small? They would play hard all day and then fall asleep on the floor watching television. But you did not leave them on the floor. Because you loved your children, you would pick them up, carry them to their rooms, and tuck them into their beds. The next morning, much to their surprise, they would wake up in their own rooms, in their own beds, because as a loving parent you had carried them there."

I looked at this man lying in the hospital bed and continued, "This is what death is like. We go to sleep in this world and we awaken in another, one where we belong because a loving God has picked us up and carried us there."

At some time or another, we all have those unexpected moments when the conversation suddenly turns to the profound. We do not have to initiate the conversation; we do not have to corner people and compel them to listen to our understanding about God. At some unexpected moment, we may be presented with an opportunity to share our faith in Jesus Christ. Will you seize the opportunity? Great things are possible in unexpected moments if we do seize the opportunity and dare to be God's disciples.

Prayer

O God, remind us of your promise always to be with us and always to love us. In Jesus' name. Amen.

Chapter Nine
The Touch Of Faith

Mark 5:25-34

Do you ever find yourself watching the television commercials? We all do at some time or another. The most successful commercials are those which touch our hearts.

There is the Hallmark commercial where the family is gathering for Christmas. A snowstorm has hit the area and Tommy, the college student, may not be able to come home.

His little brother says, "But Tommy was going to sing 'O Holy Night' with me." The commercial continues with the little brother looking out the window at the storm with no sign of Tommy. Then it's time to sing "O Holy Night" and he begins to sing all alone. As he is singing, Tommy slips in beside his little brother and begins singing with him.

The telephone company has a commercial where the wife says to her husband, "Joey called today."

"Is there something wrong?" he asks.

"No," his wife replies.

"Then why are you crying?" he asks.

The wife looks up and wipes the tears from her cheeks and says, "Joey called just to say 'I love you, Mom.'"

Then, she lays her head on her husband's shoulder and the music begins: "Reach out and touch someone."

The advertising companies know how to get the attention of the audience with these commercials. By touching the strings of the heart, they are not only making the audience aware of their product, but are also saying that using their greeting cards or long distance service, we, too, can touch someone we love.

This is what the woman in the Gospel story was trying to do as she reached out to touch the hem of Jesus' garment. The distance for this woman was not in miles, but in culture. For twelve years she had suffered with a hemorrhage and the medical science of that day could not help her. According to the Jewish law, everything she touched was defiled. The bed she slept in, the clothes she wore, the chairs she sat on — everything she touched became "unclean." Thus she was an outcast in society and no one wanted her around. The isolation made every day seem like another hopeless dawn; every sunset was stained with the pain of loneliness. She was driven to the point of despair, and that despair drove her to go into the crowd to see if she could touch the hem of the garment Jesus wore.

She had heard rumors of this Jesus. She had heard of lepers being made well ... she had heard of those blind from birth able to throw away their walking sticks ... she had heard of the crippled rising up and walking.

She had heard what Jesus did for others and she reasoned in her own mind that if she could touch him — even if it was only the hem of his garment — she would be healed of her twelve-year illness.

With this reasoning she joined the great crowd of people and began making her way toward Jesus. She struggled through the throng of people. She made no attempt to attract his attention. She only wanted to touch the hem of his robe. The closer she got, the more dense the crowd became. There were moments when she thought she would not be able to get close enough but she kept working to get closer until there he was, and she reached out with a trembling hand and touched the tip of his robe.

No one in the crowd noticed her or paid any attention to her — no one but Jesus. Recognizing a "touch of faith" from the crowd, he stopped and asked, "Who touched me?"

With a note of sarcasm in his voice, one of the disciples asked, "How should we know? Look at this crowd of people surrounding you and you ask, 'Who touched me?' "

To the disciples it was ridiculous that he would notice the touch of one person in a crowd. But Jesus stood there scanning the faces in the crowd and his eyes met hers. Something passed between them as his eyes fixed upon hers. There was no anger, no resentment, no ridicule, no scorn, or no indignation in him at her for the audacity of touching him. Instead, there was sympathy, love, and understanding as he said, "Daughter, thy faith hath made thee whole. Go in peace ... and be healed of thy plague."

I like the way one minister described this scene. He said: "This nameless woman began as a Nobody, but by touching Christ she became Somebody and in the receiving of his mercy represents Everybody who has faith in him."

Perhaps you too have felt like a nameless nobody in the crowd. Perhaps, just perhaps, you need to push your way through the midst of the crowd and get close enough to reach out to Christ. Reach out in faith and touch him and it will have a tremendous impact in your life just as it did for that woman of long ago.

I. The Touch Of Faith Brings A Change In Your Life

The woman who worked her way through the multitude of people to touch the hem of the robe of Christ was changed. With trembling fingers she had touched him. In that instance, she felt a change take place within her. She touched him in faith and a new sense of strength and vitality filled her body.

But notice what she did — she retreated back into the crowd. The disciples paid no heed to her; she did not seek the attention of the crowd. She had touched him in secret and in trembling haste. She felt the change come into her but it would have remained a secret had Jesus not asked, "Who touched me?"

One thing this story seems to say is that the touch of faith can bring a thrilling change within your life without catching the attention and the excitement of the world. There are the Apostle Pauls who catch the attention and excitement of the world when they have life-changing encounters on their "roads to Damascus." There are the Martin Luthers who gain worldwide recognition when touched by faith and deliberately take stands that polarize the world. There are the Jonathan Edwardses, John Wesleys, Billy Sundays, and Billy Grahams whose lives are so changed they devote themselves to proclaiming the gospel.

However, there are some faintly average people in life who make mistakes — who give in to what's wrong and it is called "sin" — but, by and large, they travel down the middle of the road and at some point reach out and touch the hem of his garment. This touch of faith brings a change in their everyday existence and it influences all areas of their lives. There is no dramatic, earth-shaking change. It is a change that may go unnoticed by the crowd — but Jesus notices it. Jesus is aware of lives that have been touched by faith.

I have been reading a short biography of Dag Hammarskjöld, the former Secretary-General of the United Nations. What was not widely known, until after his death in 1961, was the significance of faith in his life.

A friend, as well as his lawyer, from Sweden, began to dispose of his personal effects at his apartment in New York. Beside the bed was found a document, the contents no living person knew, simply marked "personal." When this document was examined, it was discovered to cover a period of 36 years and contained literary jewels ranging from sketches of men, to countryside scenes, to psychological self-probings. Even more remarkable was the discovery that these personal notes also constituted a private spiritual diary. It recorded his groping but finally successful journey into faith. It was a side of Hammarskjöld that the public had not known. Some close friends, themselves antireligious, were startled to discover just how much effect his faith had had on his public life.

One entry in his personal diary spoke eloquently of how the touch of faith brought a change in his life: "I don't know Who — or — What put the question, I don't know when it was put. I don't even remember answering. But at some moment I did answer yes to Someone — or Something — and from that hour I was certain that existence is meaningful and that therefore, my life, in self-surrender (to him) had a goal ..."

The touch of faith is not always a dramatic, earth-shaking encounter. In fact, for many of us it is simply a moment when we dare to reach out toward him and touch the hem of his garment. When we pull back our hand the crowd has not noticed — but we know we have been changed and so does Jesus.

II. The Touch Of Faith Indicates God Is Interested In You

This woman with a twelve-year sickness had the courage to reach out to Jesus. She had no purse filled with gold — only faith.

She did not meet him in the Temple for she was barred from the Temple because of her illness and her clothes would have caused her embarrassment. She did not request a private audience with the Christ — she was simply one in a crowd. Yet she reached out and touched him in faith — a blind, desperate, believing faith.

And what did Jesus do? Ignore her? Walk on and not pay any attention to this insignificant woman? No! Jesus stopped! The touch of one anonymous woman in a crowd halted Jesus and he asked, "Who touched me?" There is something significant here. The touch of faith has the power to stop Jesus in his tracks, to make him aware of your problems, your pain, and your needs.

You may think it impossible — that God is surely not interested in you. You may even agree with Mark Twain who used to say: "God doesn't even know we are here and if he does, he doesn't care." You may feel that God is not interested in you. But Jesus stopped to help a nameless woman who touched the hem of his garment and he is just as interested in you.

I like the old story about the census taker waking up a man of Irish descent in Boston one Saturday morning. The census taker asked his questions as the Irishman rubbed his eyes, yawned, and took a few minutes to wake up. The census taker worked his way down the chart of questions, like name, address, religious preference, and place of employment. Then he asked, "How many children to you have?"

By his reaction, it was plain to see that the Irishman liked to talk about his children. With a gleam of a loving father in his eyes, he said: "Well, there's Patrick, Jr., and Catherine and Sean and Donald and Mary Kathleen and Elizabeth and ..."

The census taker interrupted and said, "I don't need their names! I just need the number."

The Irishman fixed a glare upon the census taker and said, "Sir, I'll have you know that every one of me children has got a name. We ain't got around to numbering them yet!"

Just as that Irish father was interested and concerned about each of his children, so is God. We are not insignificant to God because God is interested in us ... God cares about us ... God knows us and our needs.

Just as that woman long ago needed to reach out and touch Jesus in faith, so do we. We all have different reasons for reaching out to Jesus Christ. Some of us need to reach out for forgiveness. Some of us need to reach out for courage to face difficult problems in our lives. Some of us need to reach out for strength in overcoming temptations we know are wrong but are so appealing to us. Some of us need to reach out for guidance as we make decisions about our lives.

What is your reason? Look inside your own heart and life. Then, reach out your trembling hand ... reach out and touch the hem of his garment ... reach out to Jesus Christ. And as you do, I believe he will say to you as he did to that woman long ago: "... your faith has made you whole...."

Prayer

O God, give us the courage to reach out to Jesus and the faith to know that he is already reaching out to us. In his name. Amen.

Chapter Ten
The Touch Of Human Kindness

Matthew 8:14-15

It was a cold and icy day in January as a gasoline truck made its way toward its first stop. Just as the truck rounded a curve, the semi jackknifed and skidded off the road and into a parking lot. A 23-year-old woman was getting into her car just as the semi skidded into it. The car turned over onto its side ... the young woman was pinned underneath ... and the gasoline spilling from the truck caught fire. The truck and the car shielded the young woman from the flames, but the heat was intense. The heat was making the paint on the car blister. There was a danger of the gasoline truck exploding.

The first firefighters on the scene immediately started spraying water on the young woman to keep her from burning. But she was frightened. She pleaded for someone to get her out, but the firemen had to wait for additional equipment to help free her from the wreckage.

While they were waiting, one of the firemen crawled in to tell her the situation. She became hysterical with fear when she was told she would have to wait. So the fireman reached out his hand and said to her: "Take hold of my hand. Whatever happens, I won't leave you."

So, with an inferno burning only a few feet away and the very real danger of an explosion, the firefighter lay there holding the hand of a trapped and frightened young woman.

Finally, the crane arrived. Although it had seemed to be an eternity, only twelve minutes had passed. The crane lifted the car up a little bit. The woman was dragged to freedom and rushed to the hospital.

Later, in the hospital, a news reporter asked the young woman, "What do you remember the most about being trapped under that car with the fire raging only a few feet away?"

Without hesitation, the young woman said: "The thing I remember the most is that fireman risking his life and staying there with me to hold my hand. His hand is what kept me sane. His hand was the touch of human kindness that calmed my fears."

What had impressed this young woman the most was not the overwhelming fear gripping her heart ... it was not the loneliness of being trapped ... it was not the promise that help was on its way. The thing that impressed this young woman the most was the touch of someone's hand upon hers.

The touch of human kindness has a powerful impact upon everyone's life because all of us feel lonely at times. All of us have those times when we are afraid. All of us have a need to feel the touch of human kindness upon our lives.

I wonder if we really appreciate how essential the touch of human kindness is to life. Dr. Samuel Johnson said: "Kindness may not be all the creed this world needs, but it does need it desperately."

The absence of simple kindness is responsible for a great deal of our unhappiness. There is a lot of sin in this world, but there is an even greater absence of sympathy and understanding. So often we get caught up in the rush of life and become so engrossed in our own little wishes and wants that we develop an impersonal, unfeeling attitude toward people. We become so wrapped up in our own world that we keep other people at arm's length and never really notice those opportunities to reach out with the touch of human kindness.

But Jesus never lost sight of the individual need to feel the touch of human kindness. He not only preached to the multitude, fed the thousands, and healed lepers and the sick that came to him by the thousands, but he also had an instinctive feeling for the needs of the individual. His interest in people was personal. It was his quickness in understanding, it was his instinctive feeling that compelled him to reach out and touch people with kindness.

I like this Scripture passage in Matthew. It very clearly portrays the touch of human kindness that seemed to be instinctive with Jesus. "On entering the house Jesus noticed that Peter's mother-in-law was down with a fever."

Jesus had a quick eye. He was sensitive to a need and he saw it when he entered the house. He was in Capernaum for a rest and was returning from the synagogue. There was not a crowd of people around him — only his disciples. He did not have to impress anyone and yet, when he entered the house, he saw that Peter's mother-in-law was down with a fever. (The fever she had was most likely malaria which was very common to that part of the world.) Here was a woman tossing with a fever, and Jesus reached out and touched her because he cared about her. He touched her with the "quinine of kindness."

How many times from the life and ministry of Jesus do we learn that the touch of human kindness is important? The Good Samaritan was not the one who saw a need and passed by, but the one who stopped and administered the healing touch. The woman in the crowd who touched the hem of his garment was surprised that Jesus would show her any kindness. Children seemed to know instinctively that Jesus had time for them. One day when they tried to go to him, the children were stopped by the disciples. But Jesus said: "Suffer the little children to come unto me, do not hinder them." According to Jesus, the last judgment itself turns on whether a person has the touch of human kindness. It is little acts of kindness like feeding the hungry, clothing the naked, giving a drink to someone who is thirsty, or visiting those who are sick or in prison. All these acts of kindness will be important on that day.

With the examples of Jesus so clear and his teaching so explicit, it is strange that more attention has not been given to this touch of human kindness. Maybe we need to look a little more closely at the life and teaching of Jesus. If we do, we will discover the touch of human kindness is the hallmark of real faith.

I. The Touch Of Human Kindness Opens Our Eyes To See Those In Need

As soon as Jesus walked into Peter's house, he saw someone in need and reached out to help her. In our more honest moments, we have to confess that we have blinders on when it comes to seeing people in need. We may see them and their need, but we have problems of our own and, thus, shrink from any human contact that might require us to become involved.

A church leader, James Cox, who is Professor of Preaching at a seminary in Kentucky, told about walking through an airport terminal one day. He was scheduled to speak to a conference meeting of about 500 ministers and their wives. His plane had been delayed. Now he had to rush to make his speaking engagement on time. Mentally, he was going over his speech while walking briskly through the airport terminal to grab a taxi. Suddenly a man with an outstretched hand approached him for help. The man was staggering as if drunk and Dr. Cox hurriedly walked on by because he was too busy and too late to be bothered by a drunk. Dr. Cox said: "Later I learned that the man I thought was drunk was actually having a heart attack, and he was reaching out to someone for help."

How many times have we been in a similar situation? How many times have we gotten so wrapped up in our own little world that we don't see those in need? We don't notice the misery of the world around us? We don't care about the injustice happening to some people? How many times have we walked on by while others were reaching out to us for help? With the fast pace we live and our own peculiar set of problems, it is easy for us to get wrapped up in ourselves. It is easy for us to walk on by. It is easy for us to ignore those opportunities where the touch of human kindness might have helped someone.

However, if we are truly to be followers of Jesus Christ, we must learn to look at the world around us through Christ-colored glasses. That means we must learn to look at the world through the eyes of Jesus Christ.

II. The Touch Of Human Kindness
Reminds Us To Treat People With Dignity

Whenever you see Jesus in the Scripture, there is one thing always clear. He treated people with a sense of dignity and respect. He accepted people as they were. Zacchaeus, a tax collector, was ridiculed and hated. Yet Jesus went home with him to share a meal. A woman taken in the act of adultery and thrown at his feet was treated as a human being in need of forgiveness. A woman of questionable character approached Jesus and some wondered why he treated her with dignity and respect. Jesus seemed to know instinctively that the greatest need for some people is to be accepted and treated with respect.

When I was a child, my grandfather would quote a little poem. It went:

> *I eat my peas with honey.*
> *I've done it all my life.*
> *It makes the peas taste funny,*
> *But it keeps them on the knife.*

Now that poem didn't make any sense to me since I had never seen anyone eat peas with a knife. However, that used to be a custom of some we would call Hillbillies. Last year, *Guideposts* magazine had a story about a woman who did eat peas with a knife. Cori Connors grew up in the Depression years. One day her father brought home a man named Henry. Henry was a hobo. Henry was hungry and had been invited to eat with the family that evening.

When the meal was served, Henry grabbed his knife and started eating his English peas. Cori and the other children at the table were astonished at Henry's ability to balance the peas on the knife. Soon, all of the children were giggling and pointing at Henry.

The father gave them a stern look to quiet them. Then he laid down his fork and picked up his knife and began attempting to eat peas with his knife. He was not nearly as successful as Henry, but he kept at it until he captured and ate every pea with his knife.

That day, Cori Connors and her whole family learned a valuable lesson. They learned that kindness was the most important of manners. They learned that accepting people for who they are is important. They learned that treating people, even those who are different from us — treating all people — with dignity is the touch of human kindness.

III. The Touch Of Human Kindness Helps Lead People To God

Sometimes the only picture some people have of God is the life you and I live. We may not be able to talk to people about the need of God in their lives, but if we keep our eyes open to be of service, we can be a living witness of God's love to those who would not listen to our words. Sometimes the action of human kindness can break down barriers and open doors that our words would never be able to budge.

Robert McCracken tells of a Methodist minister by the name of W. H. Lax who was pastor for 38 years on the east end of London. He learned one day that an old man was gravely ill and went to call on him. As soon as the sick man discovered his visitor was a minister, he refused to talk to him. The minister was an unwelcome guest. While trying to sustain a conversation, Reverend Lax noted the dreariness of the room and the pitifully small fire, and he suspected that provisions had run low.

When he left, he passed by a butcher shop and had two lamb chops sent to the house. He called again a few days later and although the old man was still far from talkative, he was friendlier. On the way home, the minister again left an order of two lamb chops with the butcher. By the third visit there was a change: the old man was even more friendly and even asked the minister to read Psalm 23 and have a word of prayer with him.

A preaching engagement took the minister out of town for a few days. When he returned he was informed that the old man had died and had left a message. The message, scribbled on a piece of paper, said: "Dear Reverend, I want you to know that I'm going home to God. I want you to know that it wasn't your preaching that changed me, it was those lamb chops. They told me that you really cared. Your friend."

Yes, the touch of human kindness can break down barriers of misunderstanding. The touch of human kindness can help lead people to God by allowing them to see something of God's love shining through your life. The touch of human kindness is one of the hallmarks of our faith. Can others see something of God in your life? Is the touch of human kindness a hallmark of your faith?

Remember what Jesus said: "Inasmuch as you did it to one of the least of these ... you did it to me."

Prayer

O God, teach us the art of being kind to all people simply because it is the right thing to do. In Jesus' name. Amen.

www.ingramcontent.com/pod-product-compliance
Lightning Source LLC
Chambersburg PA
CBHW071753040426
42446CB00012B/2532

Faith and Major Mental Illness